MEDICAL MARVELS

THE NEXT 100 YEARS OF MEDICINE

by Agnieszka Biskup

CAPSTONE PRESS
a capstone imprint

Graphic Library is published by Capstone Press,
1710 Roe Crest Drive, North Mankato, Minnesota 56003
www.mycapstone.com

Library of Congress Cataloging-in-Publication data is available on the Library of Congress website.
ISBN 978-1-4914-8264-3 (library binding)
ISBN 978-1-4914-8268-1 (eBook PDF)

Editor
Mandy Robbins

Art Director
Nathan Gassman

Designer
Ted Williams

Media Researcher
Jo Miller

Production Specialist
Katy LaVigne

Illustrator
Alan Brown

Colorist
Giovanni Pota

Design Element: Shutterstock: pixelparticle (backgrounds)

Printed and bound in the United States of America.

TABLE OF CONTENTS

SECTION ONE WHERE HAVE WE BEEN?

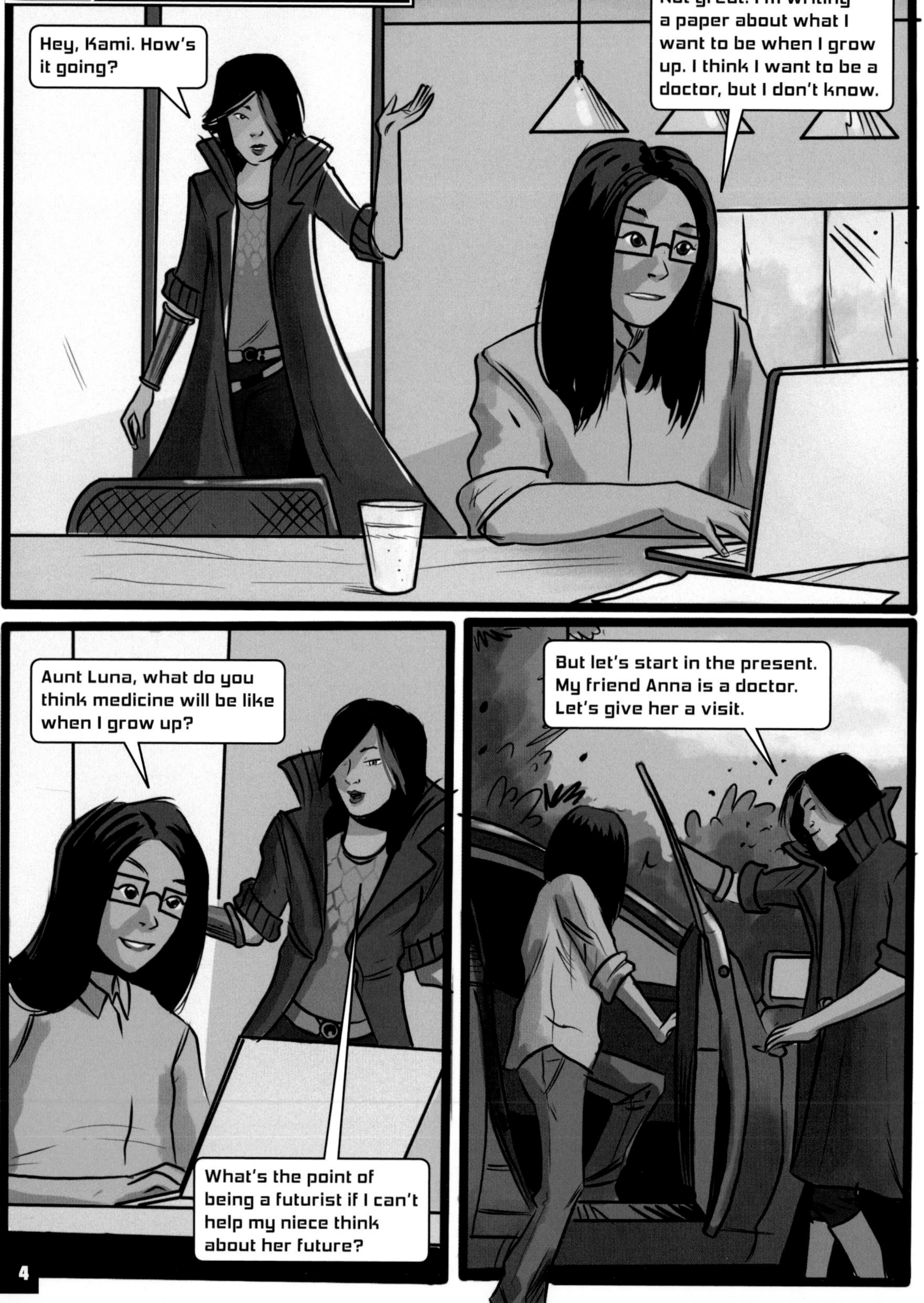

Hey, Kami. How's it going?
Not great. I'm writing a paper about what I want to be when I grow up. I think I want to be a doctor, but I don't know.
Aunt Luna, what do you think medicine will be like when I grow up?
What's the point of being a futurist if I can't help my niece think about her future?
But let's start in the present. My friend Anna is a doctor. Let's give her a visit.

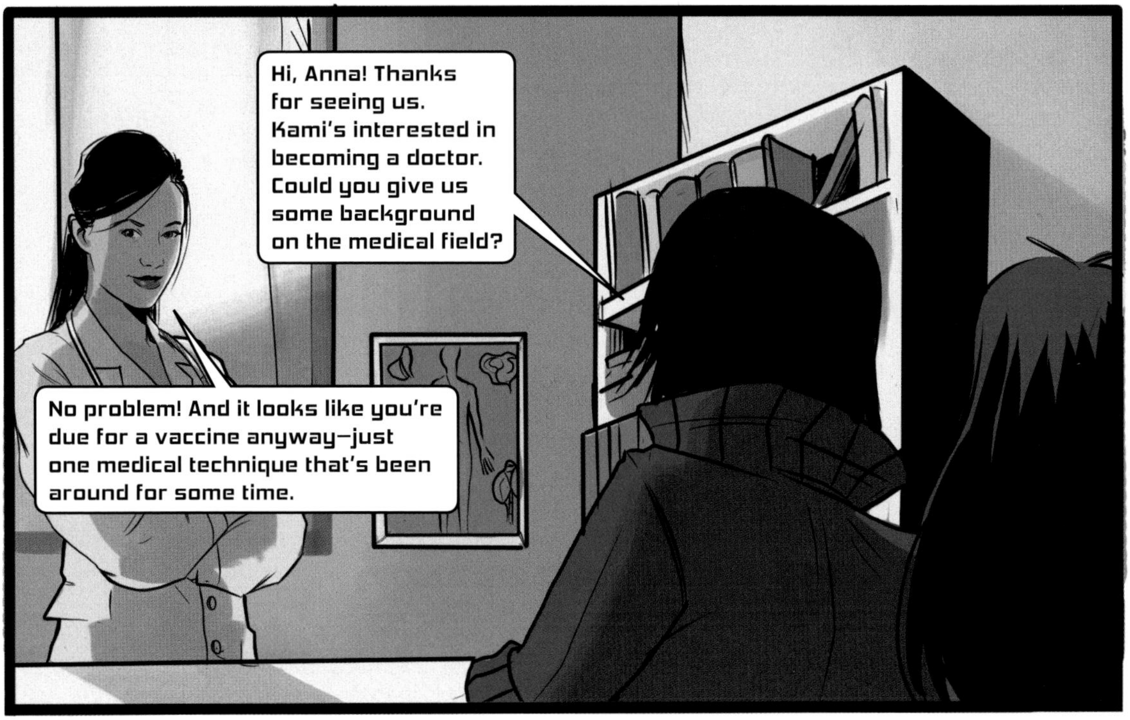
Hi, Anna! Thanks for seeing us. Kami's interested in becoming a doctor. Could you give us some background on the medical field?
No problem! And it looks like you're due for a vaccine anyway—just one medical technique that's been around for some time.

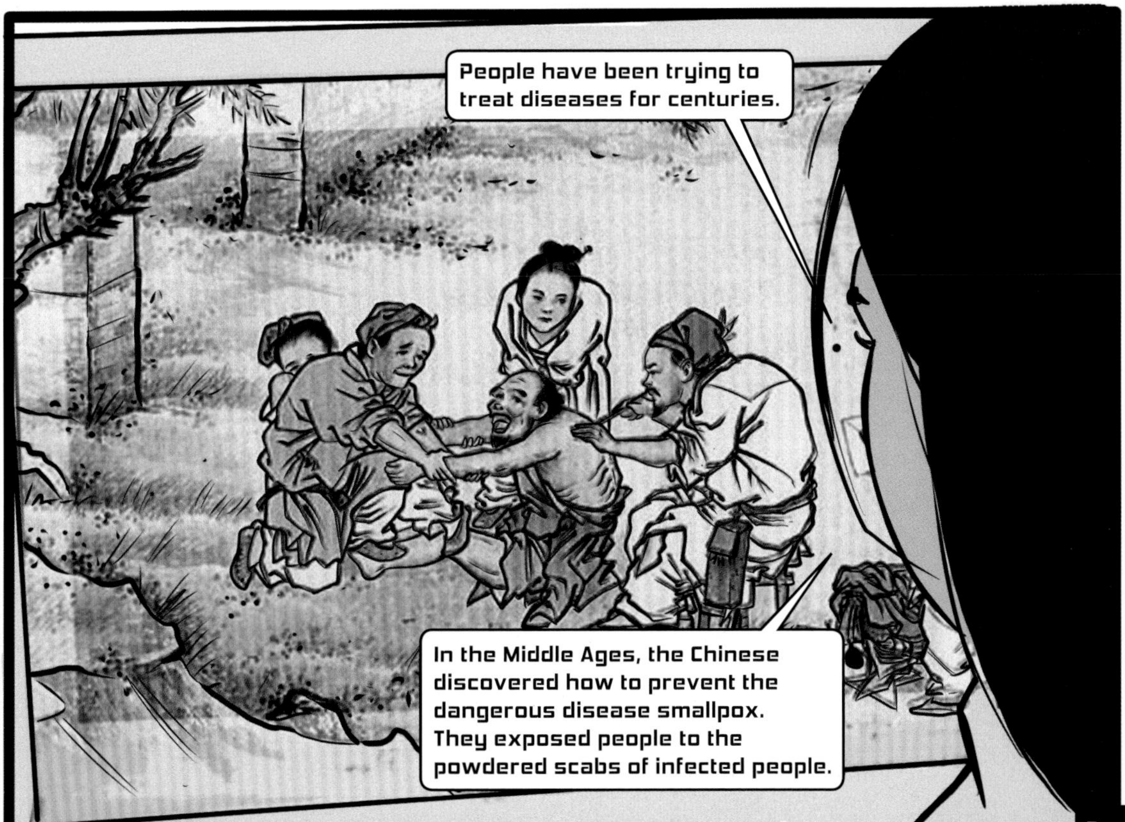
People have been trying to treat diseases for centuries.
In the Middle Ages, the Chinese discovered how to prevent the dangerous disease smallpox. They exposed people to the powdered scabs of infected people.

In the 1700s a British doctor named Edward Jenner noticed that milkmaids who'd had cowpox didn't come down with smallpox. In 1796 he treated patients with the fluid from cowpox blisters to help prevent smallpox.

Jenner called his technique a vaccine.

Medicine changes all the time. A few years ago I might have given you a shot. But today you can get some vaccines through skin patches and inhaled sprays like this.

That's awesome—I hate shots!

Ideas change, too. People used to think infectious diseases were caused by bad air until scientists discovered germs.

What exactly are germs?

They're tiny living things, such as bacteria, that can cause disease.

BACTERIA AND VIRUSES ||||||||||||||||||||||||||||||||||||

Bacteria are the smallest and simplest organisms on Earth. Like all living things, they eat, grow, and reproduce. Some bacteria are good for us, but some cause disease. Lyme disease, strep throat, and the bubonic plague are diseases caused by bacteria. Viruses, on the other hand, are tiny bundles of chemicals covered with proteins. They can only grow and multiply when they enter and take over living cells. In people, viruses cause the flu and the common cold. Some viruses also cause dangerous diseases such as smallpox, polio, and AIDS.

Scientists and doctors have come up with all sorts of medical breakthroughs to help treat and cure diseases.

Like what?

I can give you some highlights . . .

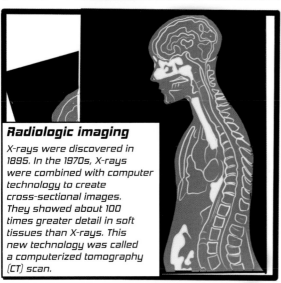

Radiologic imaging

X-rays were discovered in 1895. In the 1970s, X-rays were combined with computer technology to create cross-sectional images. They showed about 100 times greater detail in soft tissues than X-rays. This new technology was called a computerized tomography (CT) scan.

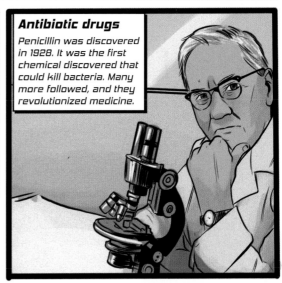

Antibiotic drugs

Penicillin was discovered in 1928. It was the first chemical discovered that could kill bacteria. Many more followed, and they revolutionized medicine.

ANTIBIOTIC RESISTANCE

Many bacterial diseases are treated with bacteria-killing drugs called antibiotics. But fast-multiplying bacteria can evolve more quickly than larger organisms. They can develop defenses against the drugs used to fight them. Today some antibiotics that once killed bacterial diseases are no longer effective against them. That's why scientists continue to search for new antibiotics.

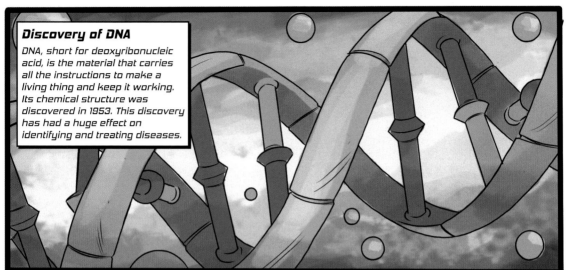

Discovery of DNA

DNA, short for deoxyribonucleic acid, is the material that carries all the instructions to make a living thing and keep it working. Its chemical structure was discovered in 1953. This discovery has had a huge effect on identifying and treating diseases.

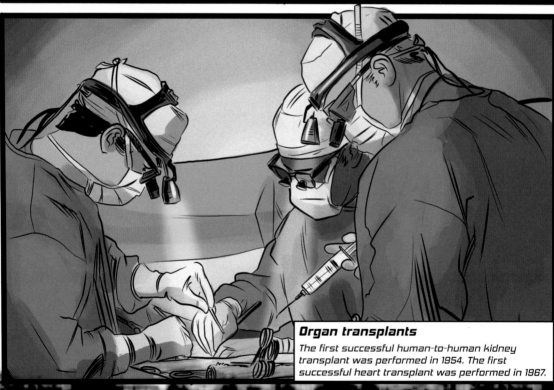

Organ transplants

The first successful human-to-human kidney transplant was performed in 1954. The first successful heart transplant was performed in 1967.

TRANSPLANT SIDE EFFECTS ||||||||||||||||||||||||||||||

Even though organ transplants save lives, they can still lead to other medical problems. People with organ transplants have to take special medicines so their immune systems don't fight the new organs. These medicines can cause health problems such as diabetes and high blood pressure, among others.

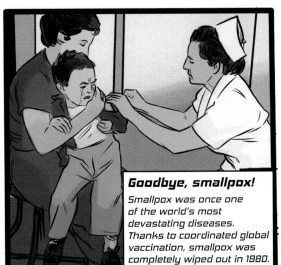

Goodbye, smallpox!

Smallpox was once one of the world's most devastating diseases. Thanks to coordinated global vaccination, smallpox was completely wiped out in 1980.

First cloned animal

Dolly the sheep was cloned in 1996. Unlike other animals, Dolly did not have a father. She was an identical copy, or clone, of her mother, created from a single cell.

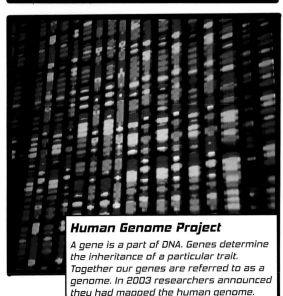

Human Genome Project

A gene is a part of DNA. Genes determine the inheritance of a particular trait. Together our genes are referred to as a genome. In 2003 researchers announced they had mapped the human genome. This breakthrough helped identify genes associated with disease. Knowing a patient's genome helps doctors provide effective care to each patient.

That was amazing—thanks for all the information!

Let me know if you need anything else!

SANITATION

Advances in sanitation and sewage removal are some of the most important medical milestones. Just providing safe drinking water and a clean environment are often the best ways to improve

WHERE ARE WE GOING NEXT?

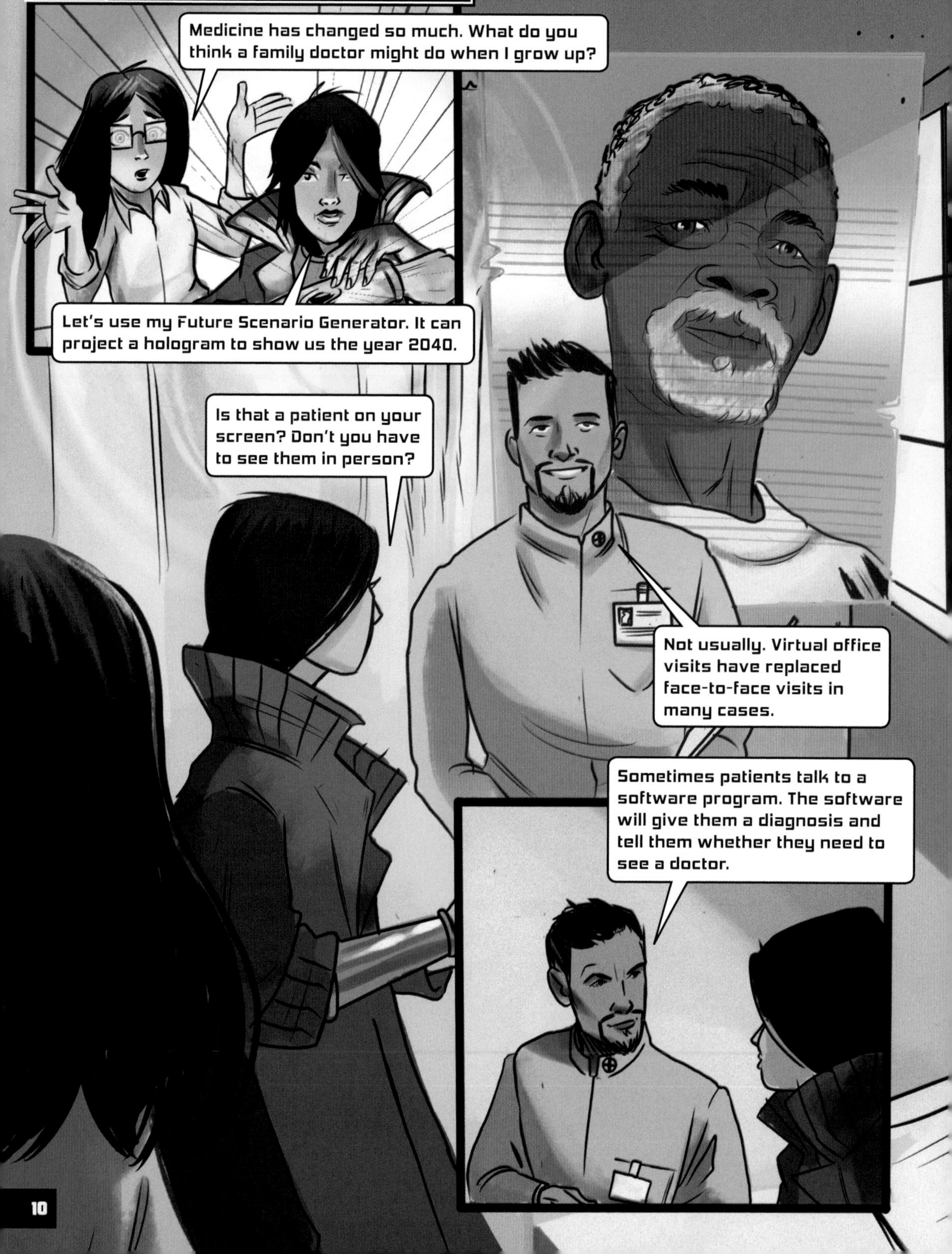
Medicine has changed so much. What do you think a family doctor might do when I grow up?
Let's use my Future Scenario Generator. It can project a hologram to show us the year 2040.
Is that a patient on your screen? Don't you have to see them in person?
Not usually. Virtual office visits have replaced face-to-face visits in many cases.
Sometimes patients talk to a software program. The software will give them a diagnosis and tell them whether they need to see a doctor.

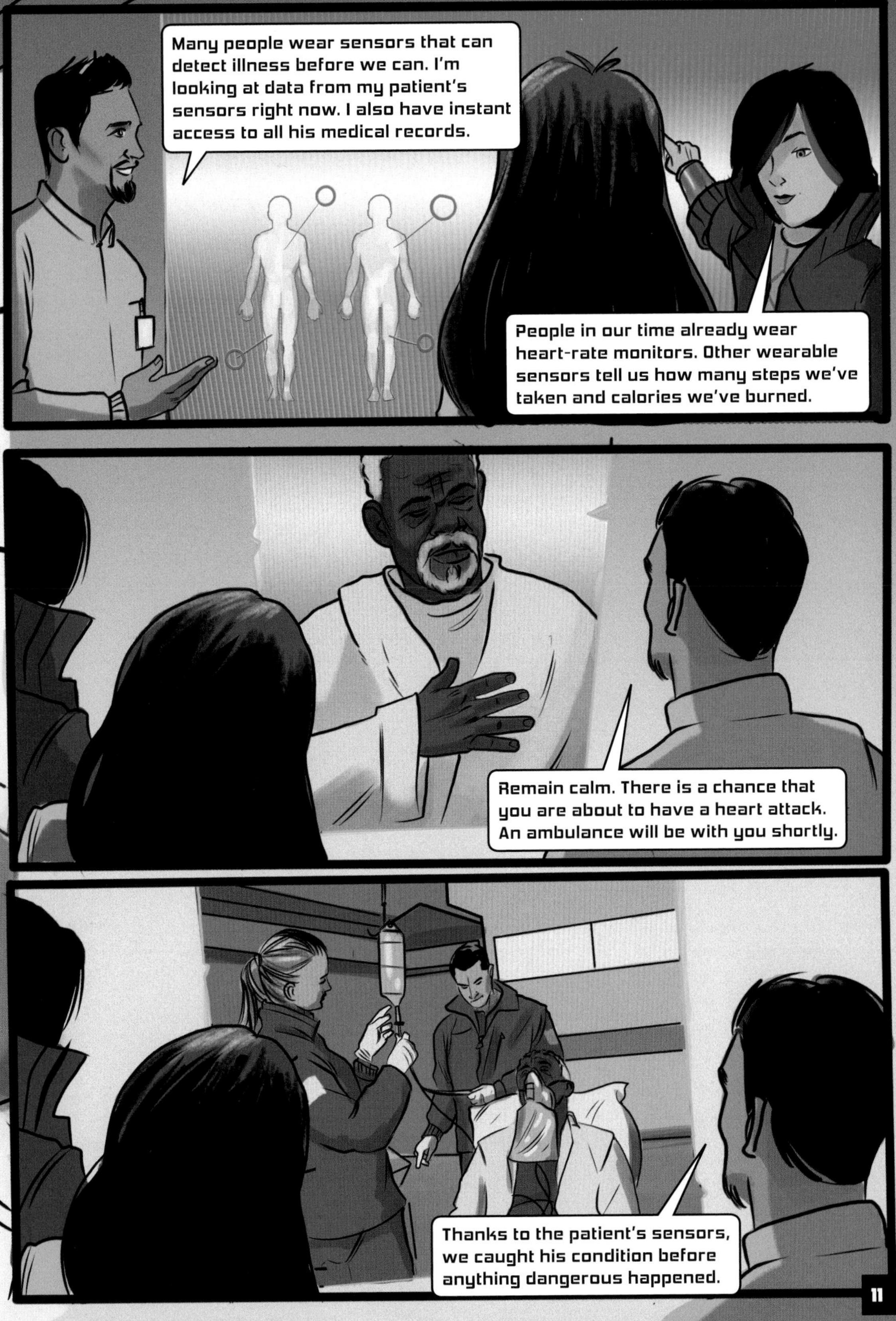
Many people wear sensors that can detect illness before we can. I'm looking at data from my patient's sensors right now. I also have instant access to all his medical records.
People in our time already wear heart-rate monitors. Other wearable sensors tell us how many steps we've taken and calories we've burned.
Remain calm. There is a chance that you are about to have a heart attack. An ambulance will be with you shortly.
Thanks to the patient's sensors, we caught his condition before anything dangerous happened.

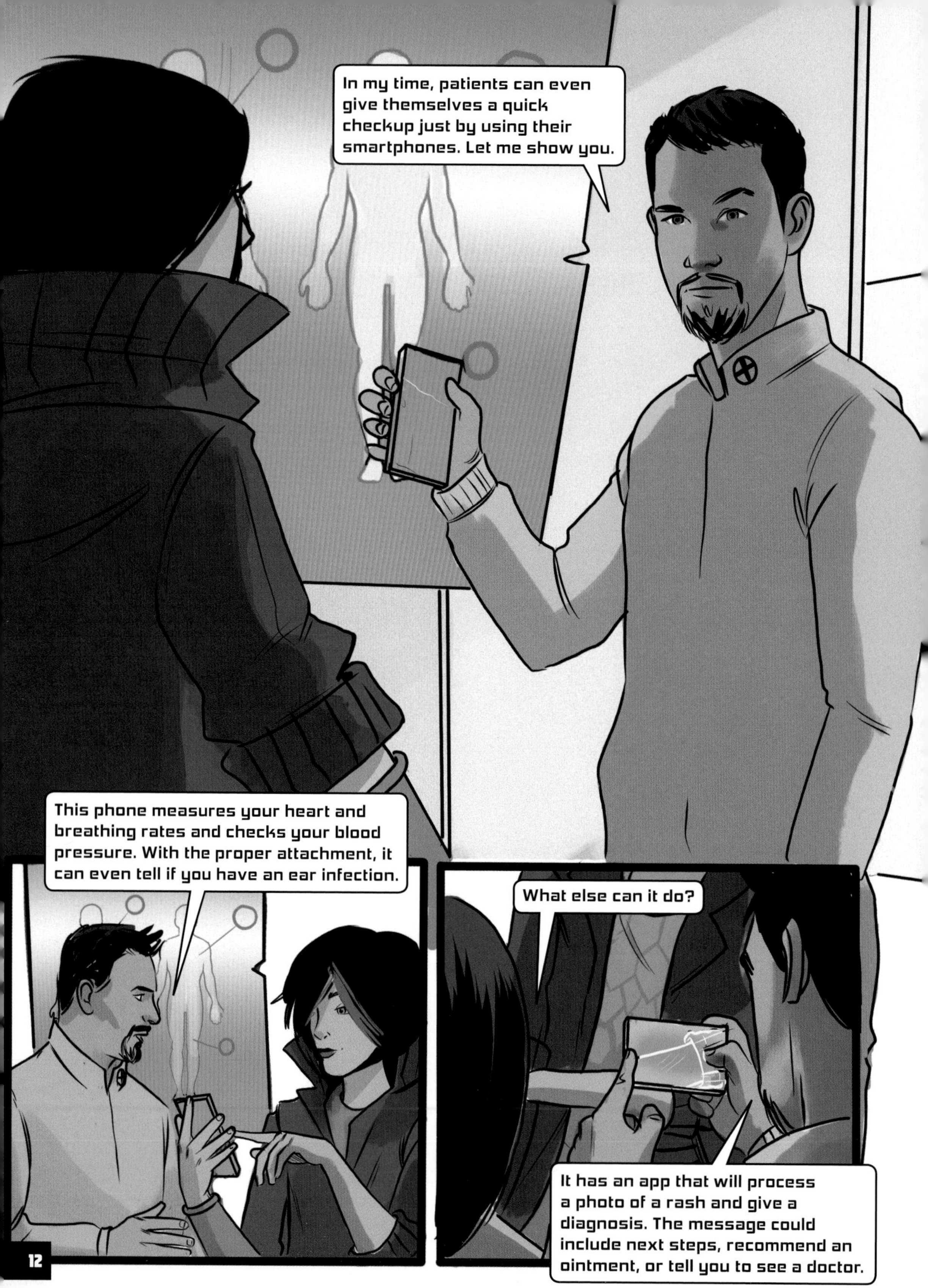
In my time, patients can even give themselves a quick checkup just by using their smartphones. Let me show you.
This phone measures your heart and breathing rates and checks your blood pressure. With the proper attachment, it can even tell if you have an ear infection.
What else can it do?
It has an app that will process a photo of a rash and give a diagnosis. The message could include next steps, recommend an ointment, or tell you to see a doctor.

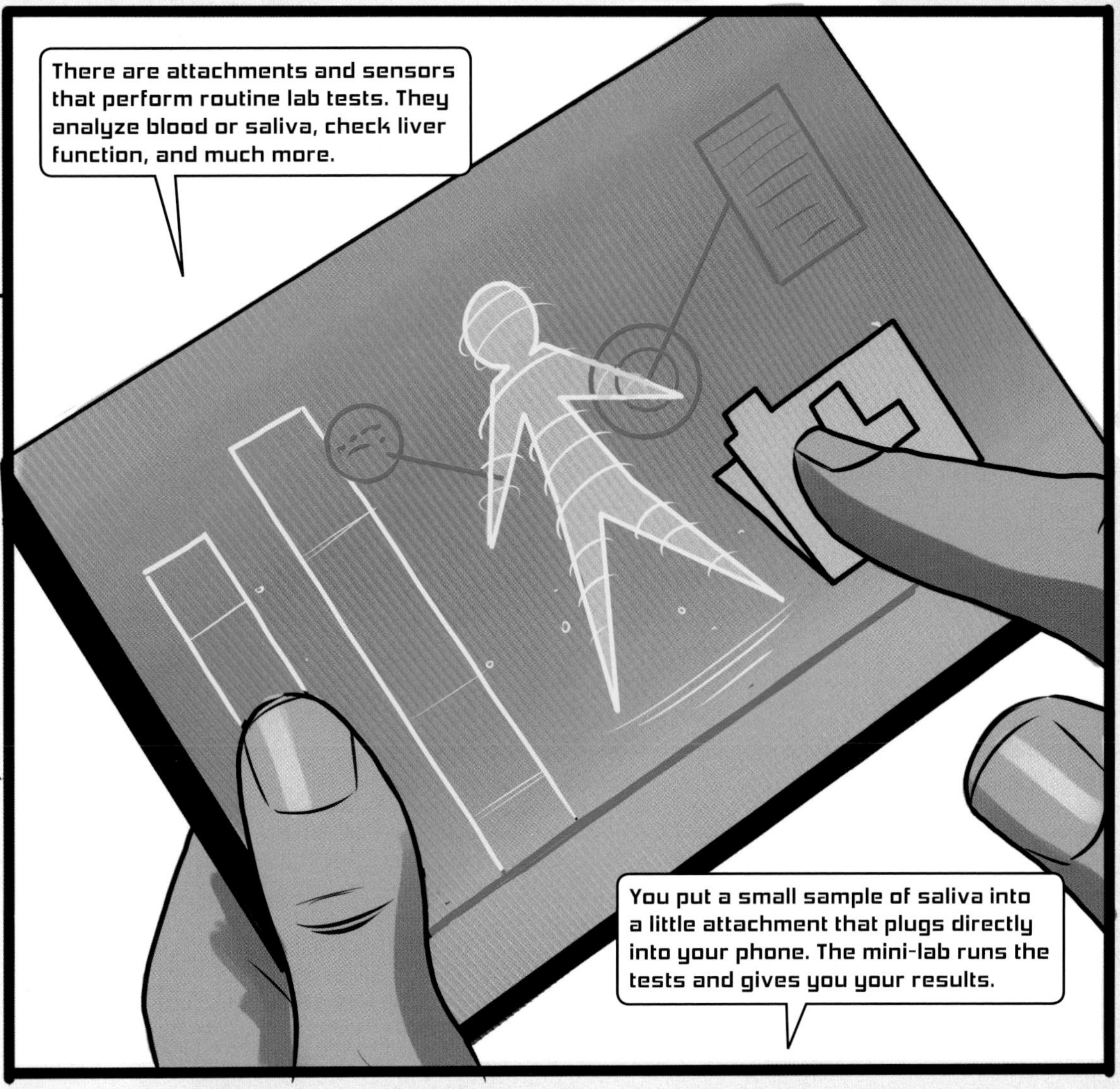
There are attachments and sensors that perform routine lab tests. They analyze blood or saliva, check liver function, and much more.
You put a small sample of saliva into a little attachment that plugs directly into your phone. The mini-lab runs the tests and gives you your results.

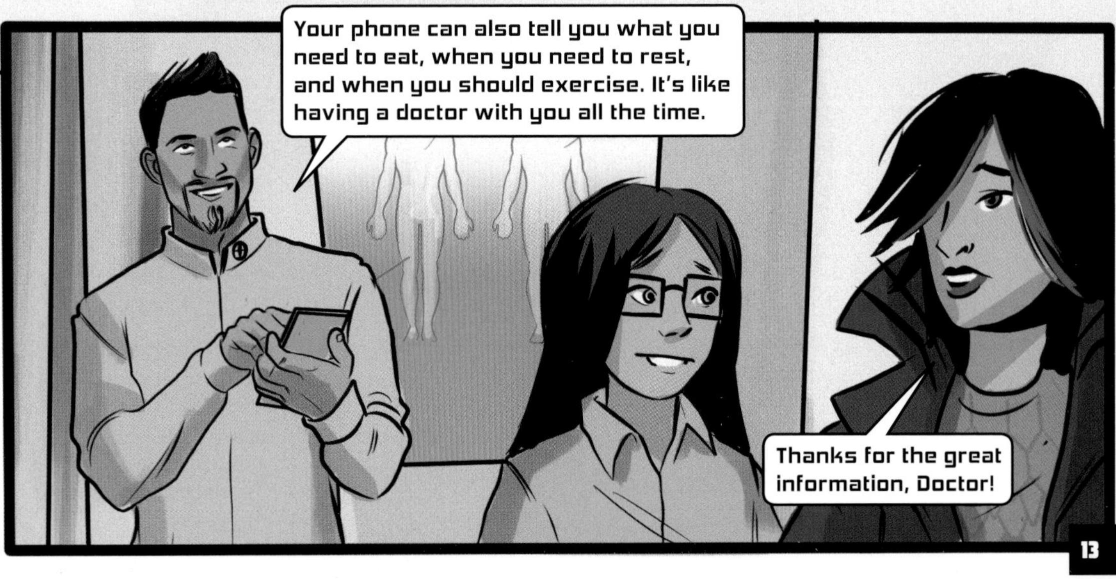
Your phone can also tell you what you need to eat, when you need to rest, and when you should exercise. It's like having a doctor with you all the time.
Thanks for the great information, Doctor!

ROBOTIC SURGERY ||||||||||||||||

Most robotic surgical systems today have a camera arm, so the surgeon can see the surgical site, and mechanical arms that have surgical instruments attached to them. The surgeon controls the arms with a computer console near the operating table. The console gives the surgeon a high-definition, magnified, three-dimensional view of what's happening. Robotic surgery lets surgeons perform delicate, complicated procedures that would be difficult to do using conventional surgery.

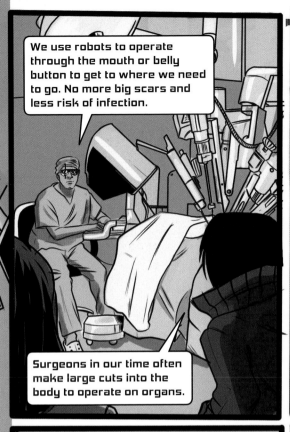

We use robots to operate through the mouth or belly button to get to where we need to go. No more big scars and less risk of infection.

Surgeons in our time often make large cuts into the body to operate on organs.

We also use robots for microsurgery. Their precision is needed for procedures such as connecting nerve fibers and tiny blood vessels.

Surgeons in our time do everything with their hands. But robots could scale down a surgeon's larger movements into microscopic ones.

What else might robots do?

They could deliver food to hospital rooms and transport equipment.

Robots could be good nurses too. They never get tired, and they're patient and reliable.

I want a robot to carry me around!

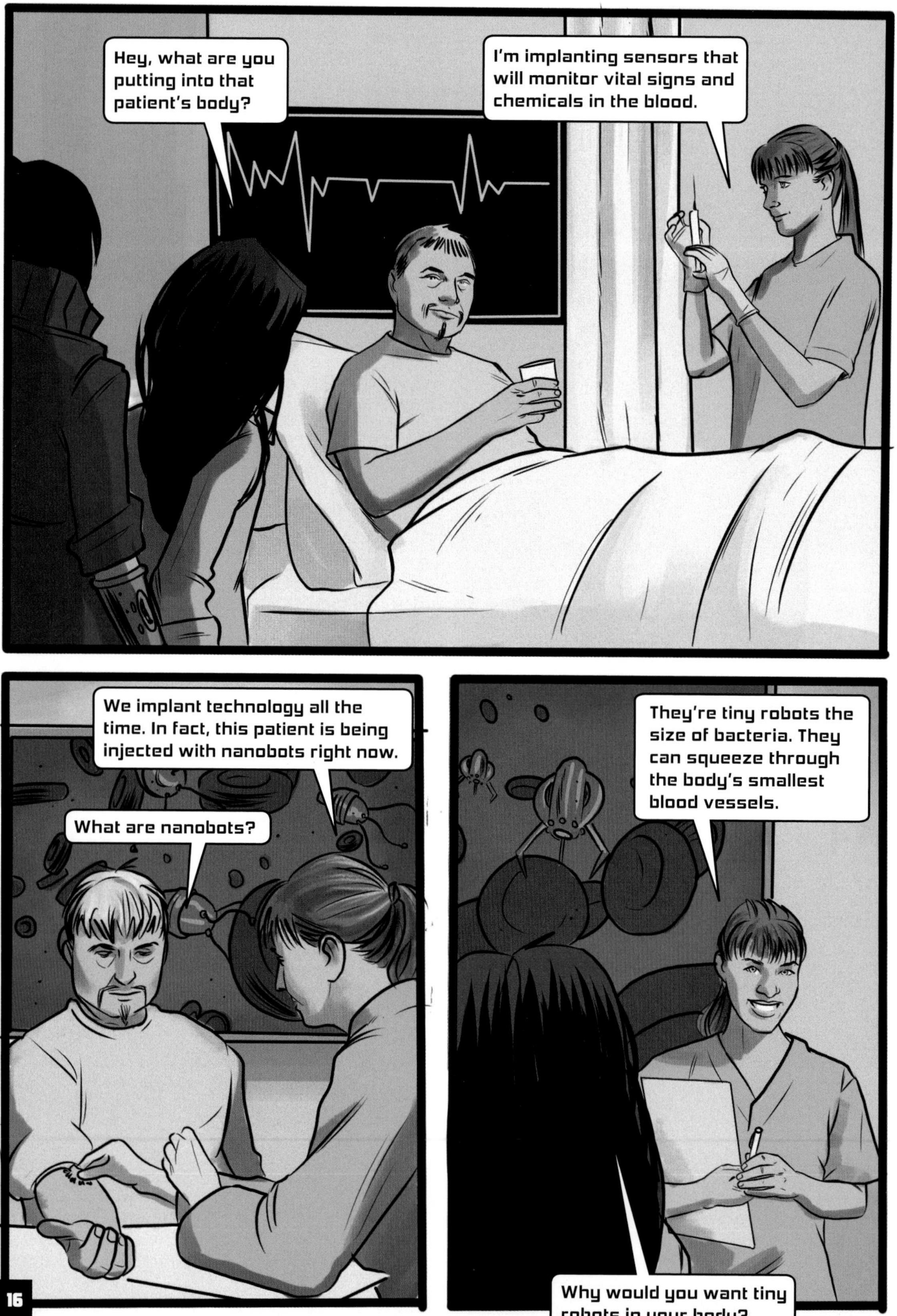
Hey, what are you putting into that patient's body?
I'm implanting sensors that will monitor vital signs and chemicals in the blood.
We implant technology all the time. In fact, this patient is being injected with nanobots right now.
What are nanobots?
They're tiny robots the size of bacteria. They can squeeze through the body's smallest blood vessels.
Why would you want tiny robots in your body?

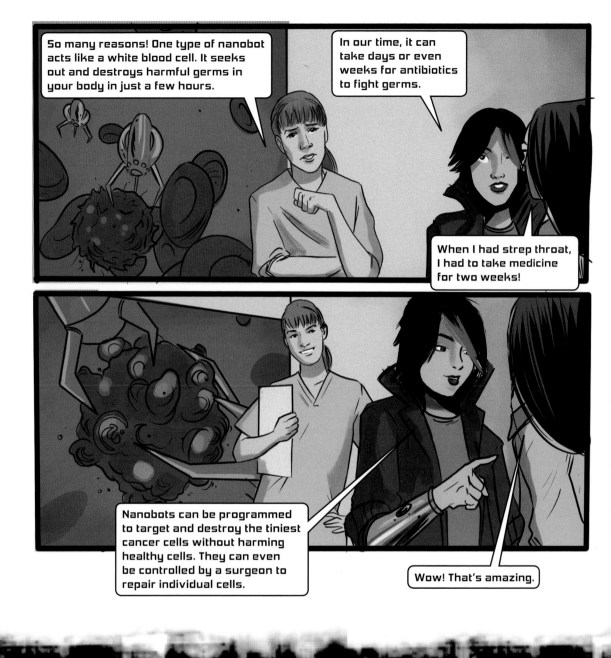

So many reasons! One type of nanobot acts like a white blood cell. It seeks out and destroys harmful germs in your body in just a few hours.

In our time, it can take days or even weeks for antibiotics to fight germs.

When I had strep throat, I had to take medicine for two weeks!

Nanobots can be programmed to target and destroy the tiniest cancer cells without harming healthy cells. They can even be controlled by a surgeon to repair individual cells.

Wow! That's amazing.

TINY ROBOT HISTORY |||||||||||||||||

The first miniaturized medical robot was a pill-sized capsule with a camera, video recorder, transmitter, and light inside. Once swallowed, the capsule sent images of the digestive

STEM CELLS AND IMPLANTS

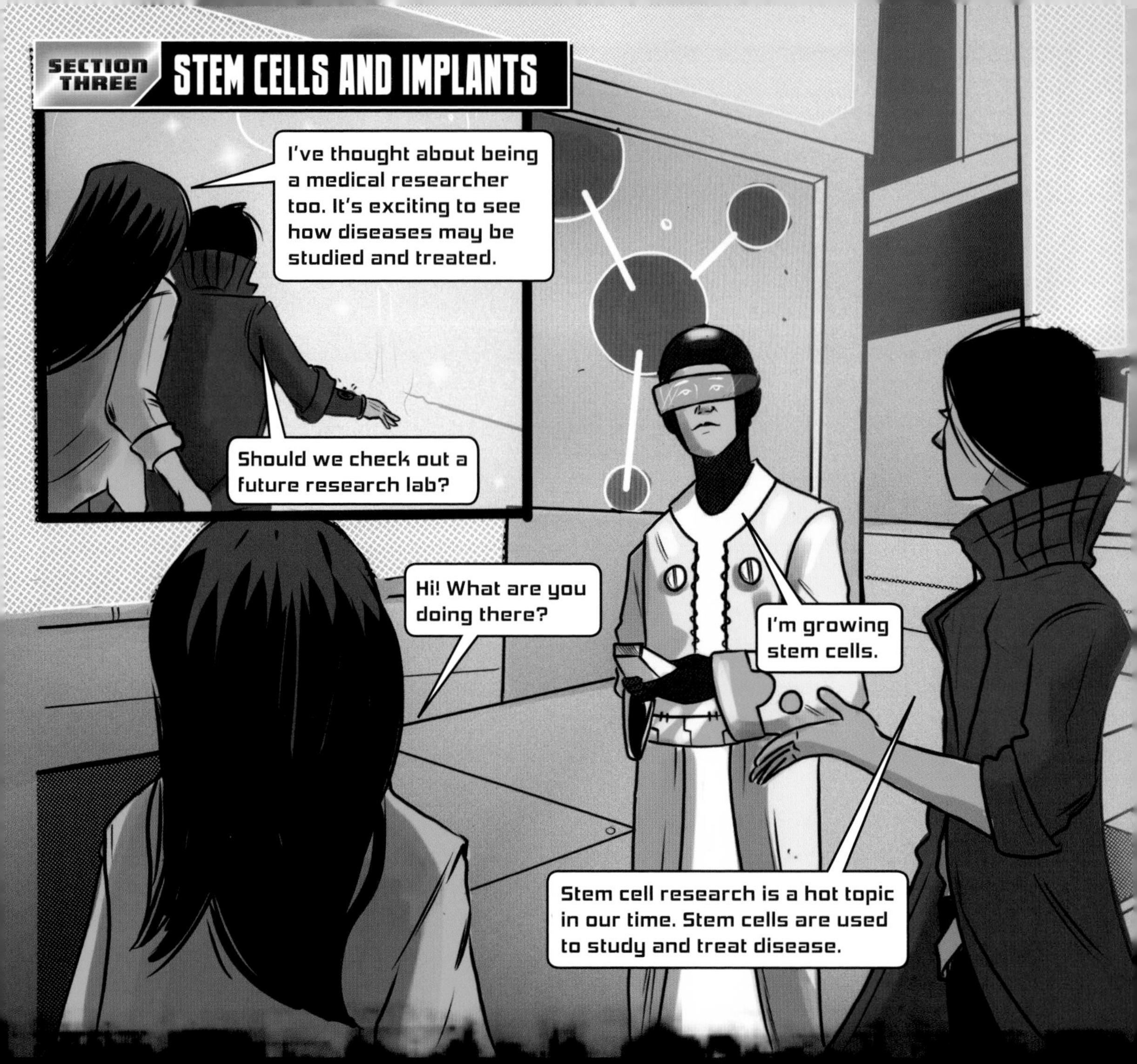

I've thought about being a medical researcher too. It's exciting to see how diseases may be studied and treated.

Should we check out a future research lab?

Hi! What are you doing there?

I'm growing stem cells.

Stem cell research is a hot topic in our time. Stem cells are used to study and treat disease.

STEM CELLS ||||||||||||||||||||||||||||

Every living thing is made up of cells, and we have many different kinds of cells in our bodies. For example, we have skin cells, brain cells, and blood cells. Most cells have specific jobs to do, and they can't do what other cells do. Stem cells are different. They can make endless copies of themselves, and they can develop into many different cell types. They are found inside people of all ages, from newborns to adults.

What are you growing them for?
We use stem cells to repair or replace tissue damaged in accidents or by disease. Stem cell therapy lets the body repair itself.
We already use stem cell therapy today when we perform bone marrow transplants. Doctors put healthy stem cells into the body to replace diseased or damaged bone marrow.
For example, in your time damaged heart valves were replaced with human-made or animal valves. With stem cell therapy, we can grow the valve using the patient's own cells.
We're using stem cells to treat diabetes, spinal cord injuries, liver disease, heart disease, and so much more. We replace damaged and destroyed cells with healthy ones that we grow in the lab.

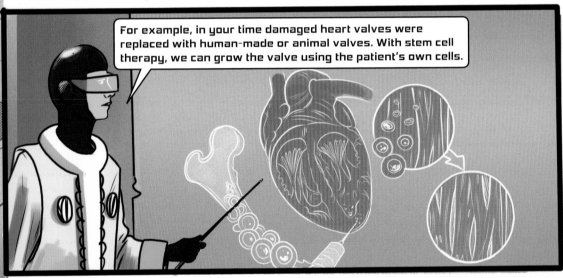

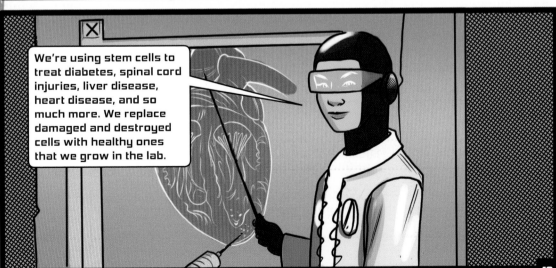

HOW A 3-D PRINTER WORKS ||||||||||||||||||||||||||||||

A 3-D printer uses a computer file to print an object one layer at a
time, not with ink, but with solid materials, such as plastic. Each new
layer is added on top of the one just printed. Just as many slices of
bread make a loaf, when a 3-D printer puts all the layers (or slices)
together, it creates the completed 3-D object.

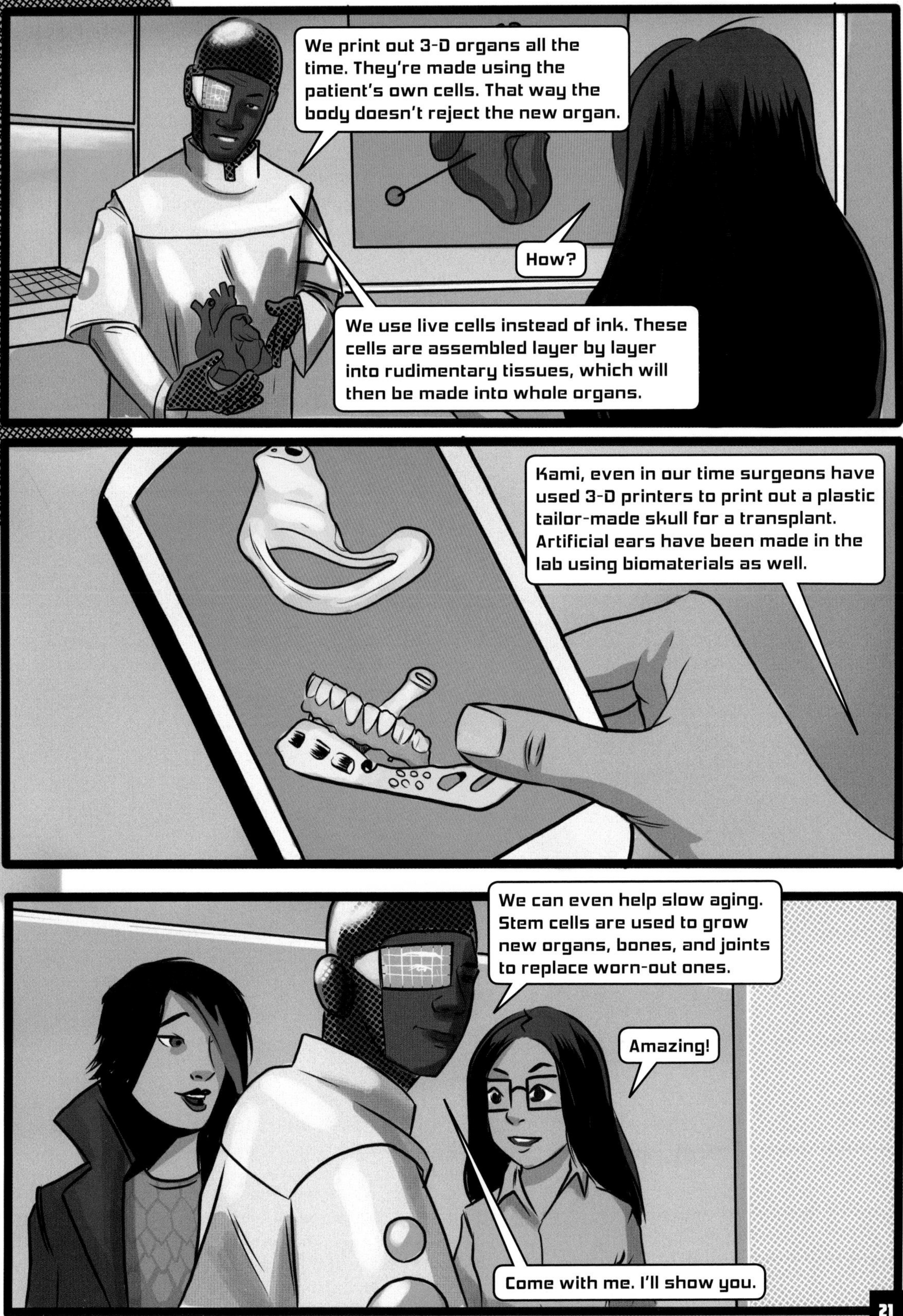
We print out 3-D organs all the time. They're made using the patient's own cells. That way the body doesn't reject the new organ.
How?
We use live cells instead of ink. These cells are assembled layer by layer into rudimentary tissues, which will then be made into whole organs.
Kami, even in our time surgeons have used 3-D printers to print out a plastic tailor-made skull for a transplant. Artificial ears have been made in the lab using biomaterials as well.
We can even help slow aging. Stem cells are used to grow new organs, bones, and joints to replace worn-out ones.
Amazing!
Come with me. I'll show you.

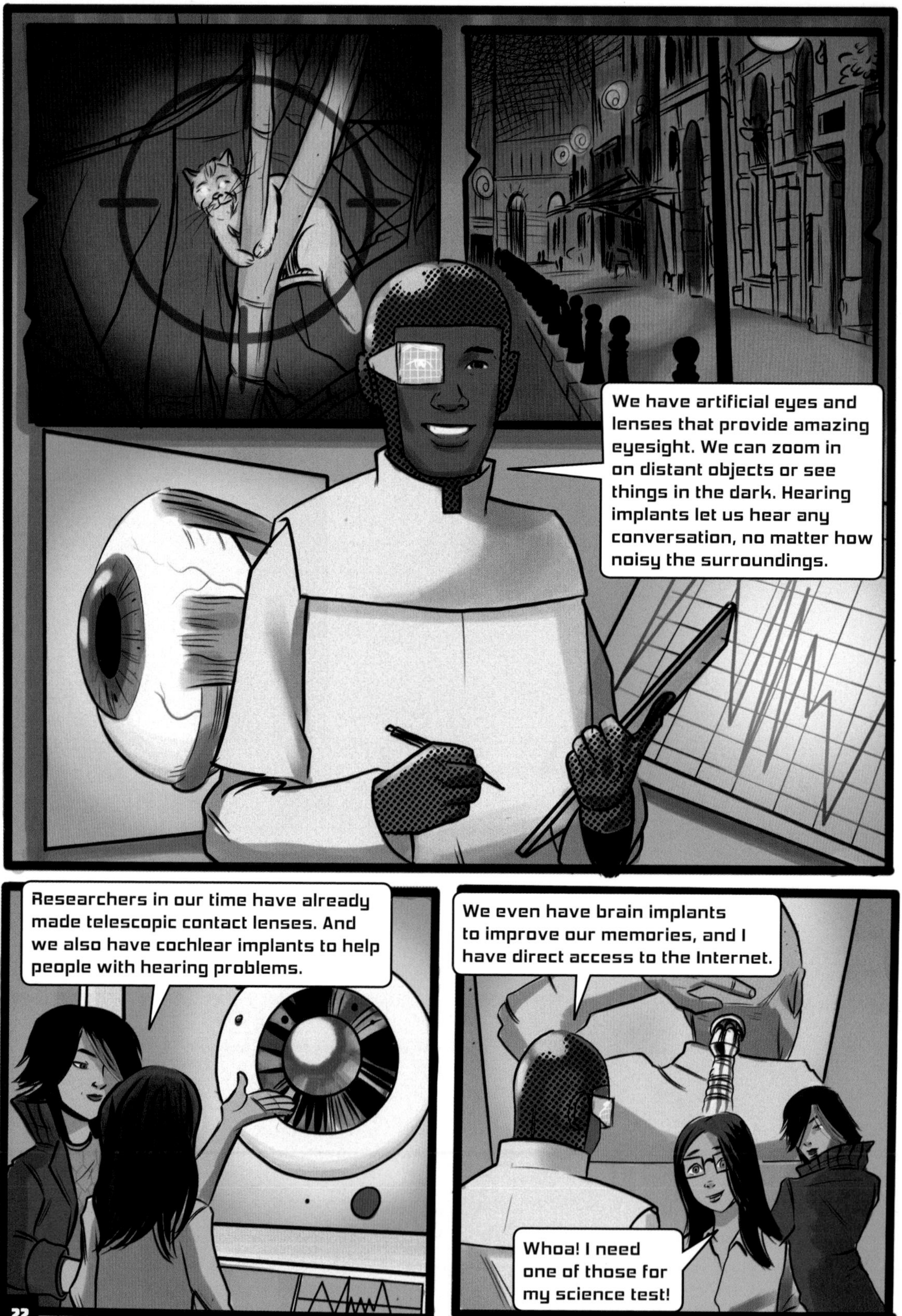
We have artificial eyes and lenses that provide amazing eyesight. We can zoom in on distant objects or see things in the dark. Hearing implants let us hear any conversation, no matter how noisy the surroundings.
Researchers in our time have already made telescopic contact lenses. And we also have cochlear implants to help people with hearing problems.
We even have brain implants to improve our memories, and I have direct access to the Internet.
Whoa! I need one of those for my science test!

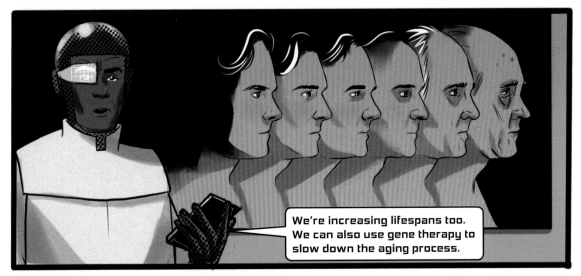

We're increasing lifespans too. We can also use gene therapy to slow down the aging process.

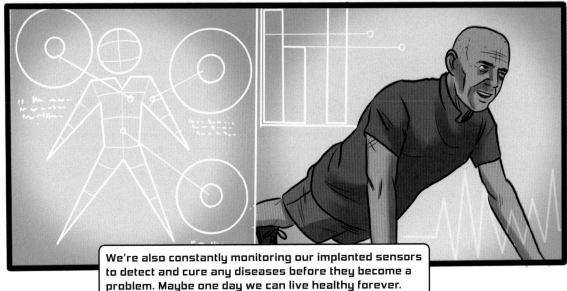

We're also constantly monitoring our implanted sensors to detect and cure any diseases before they become a problem. Maybe one day we can live healthy forever.

BIONIC EYES |||||||||||||||||||||||||||||||||||||

In 2013 the first bionic eye was approved for use in the United States. A tiny camera in a patient's glasses sends signals to an implant and then to the optic nerve. The brain uses the signals to create patterns of light. It doesn't restore normal vision, but

SECTION FOUR FARTHER IN THE FUTURE

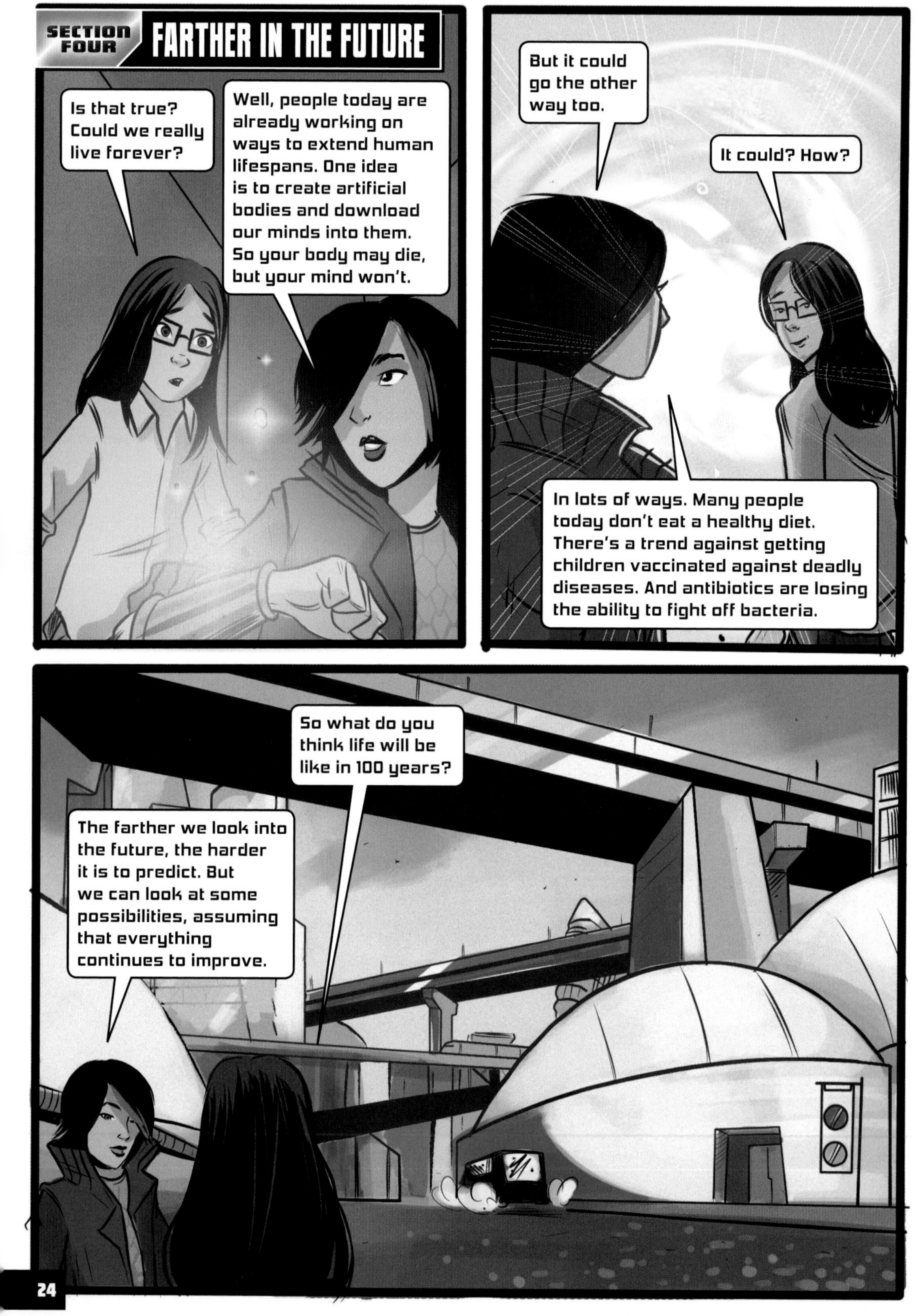

Is that true? Could we really live forever?
Well, people today are already working on ways to extend human lifespans. One idea is to create artificial bodies and download our minds into them. So your body may die, but your mind won't.
But it could go the other way too.
It could? How?
In lots of ways. Many people today don't eat a healthy diet. There's a trend against getting children vaccinated against deadly diseases. And antibiotics are losing the ability to fight off bacteria.
So what do you think life will be like in 100 years?
The farther we look into the future, the harder it is to predict. But we can look at some possibilities, assuming that everything continues to improve.

What's she doing?
I think she's trying to communicate telepathically. Sending thoughts to another brain could be like storing information on the Internet. She's sending electrical signals.
Everyone who can afford it has better brains, whether through taking medication, genetic engineering, neural implants, or prosthetic cyberbrains.
Babies in the future can be designed too. Genetic engineering lets parents choose what traits they want for their children. Genetic diseases are avoided, and intelligence and athletic ability are enhanced.
So everyone's a genius superhuman who lives forever?
It could happen. But some people probably couldn't afford it.

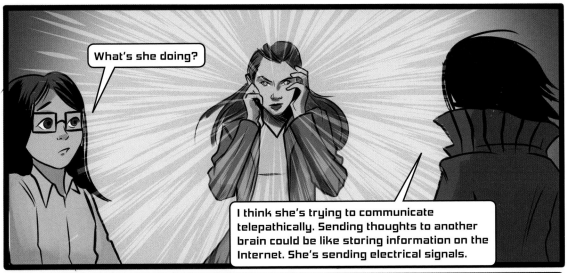

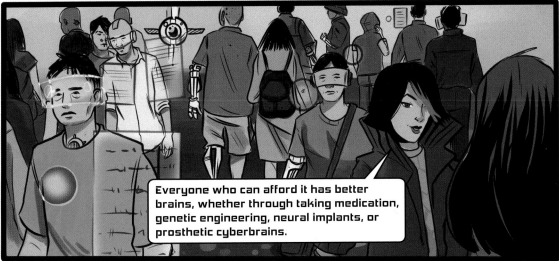

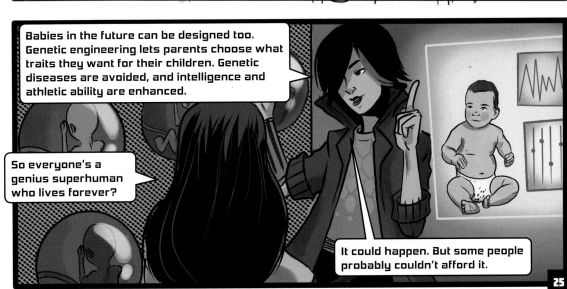

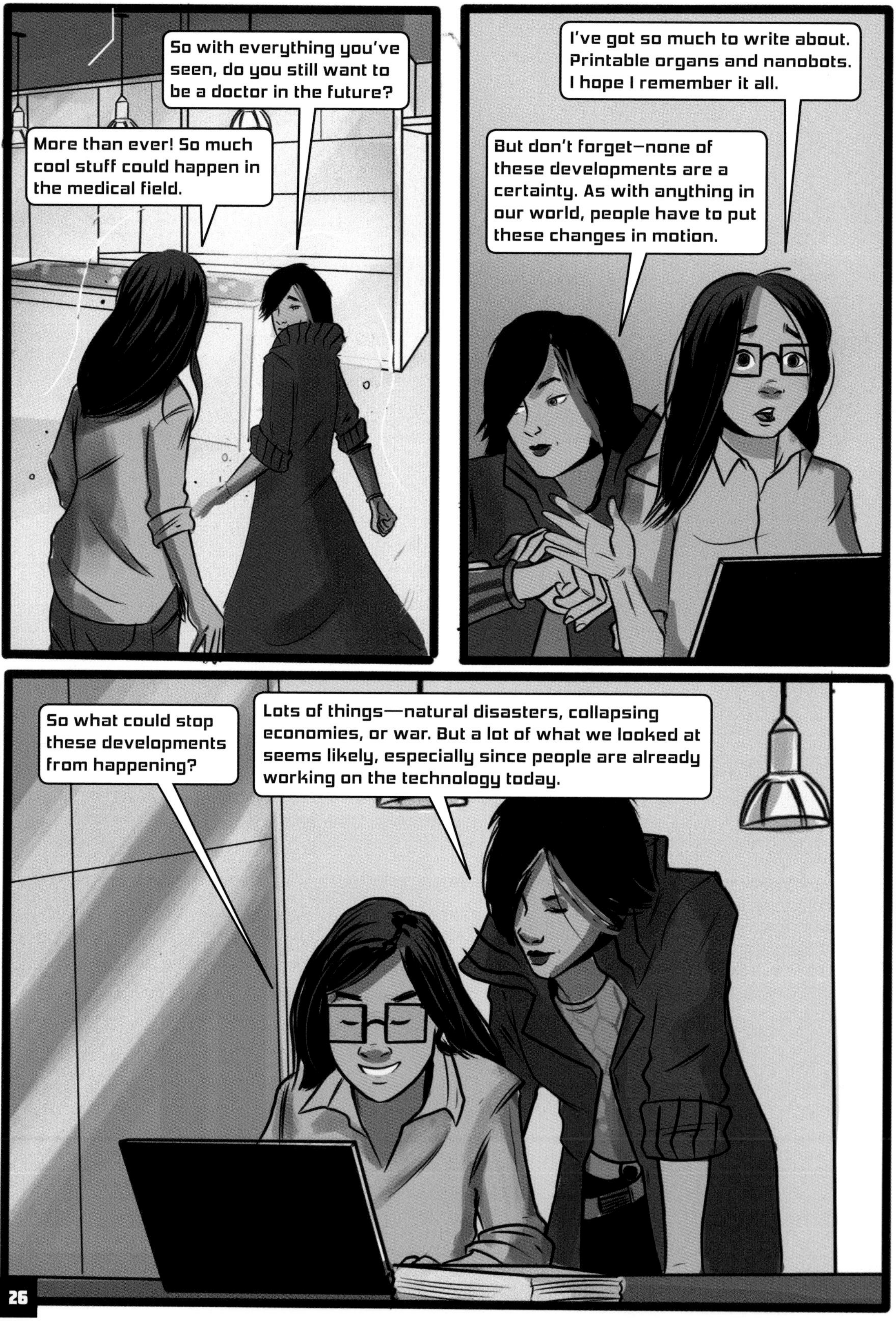
So with everything you've seen, do you still want to be a doctor in the future?
More than ever! So much cool stuff could happen in the medical field.
I've got so much to write about. Printable organs and nanobots. I hope I remember it all.
But don't forget—none of these developments are a certainty. As with anything in our world, people have to put these changes in motion.
So what could stop these developments from happening?
Lots of things—natural disasters, collapsing economies, or war. But a lot of what we looked at seems likely, especially since people are already working on the technology today.

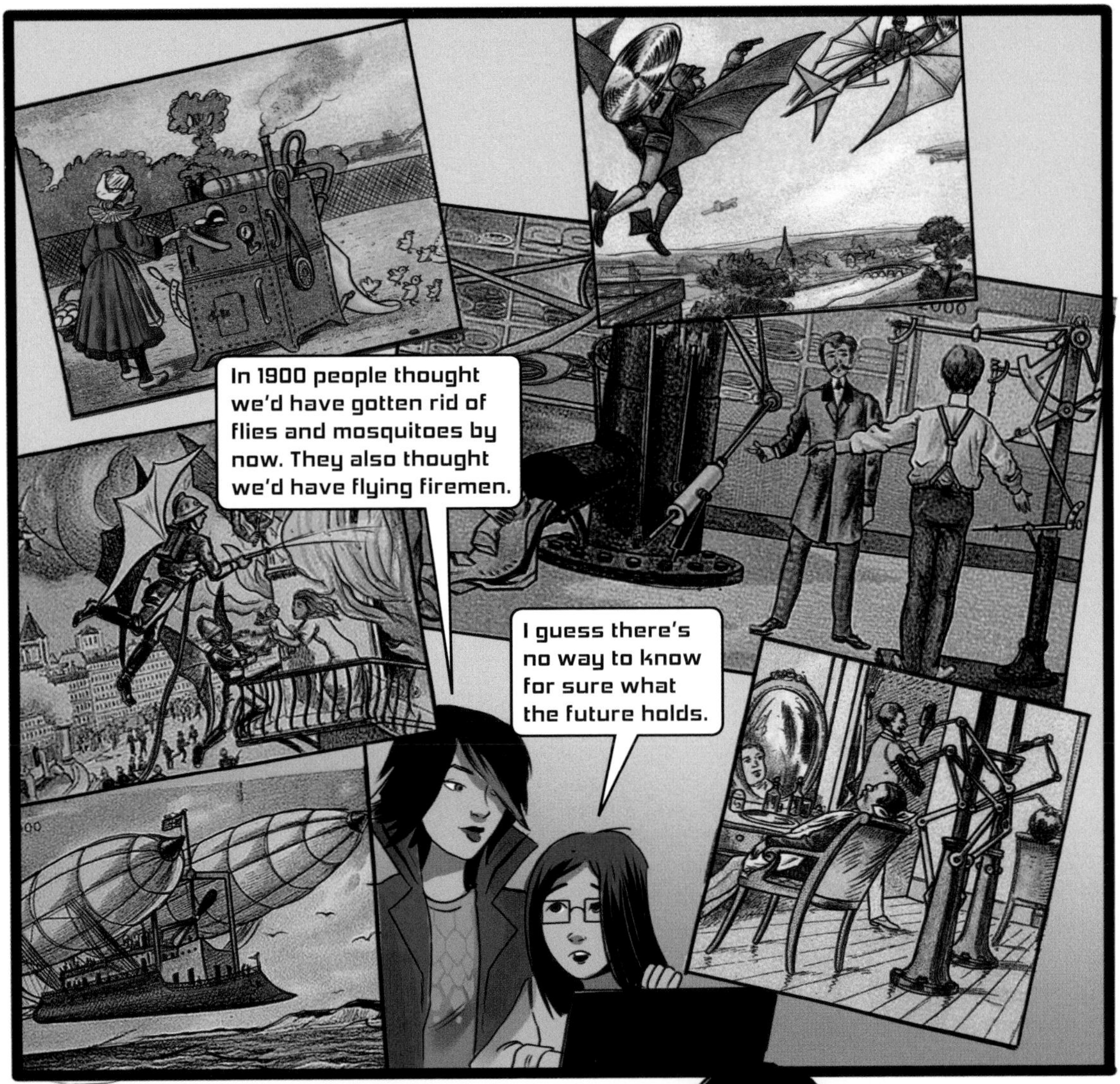
In 1900 people thought we'd have gotten rid of flies and mosquitoes by now. They also thought we'd have flying firemen.
I guess there's no way to know for sure what the future holds.

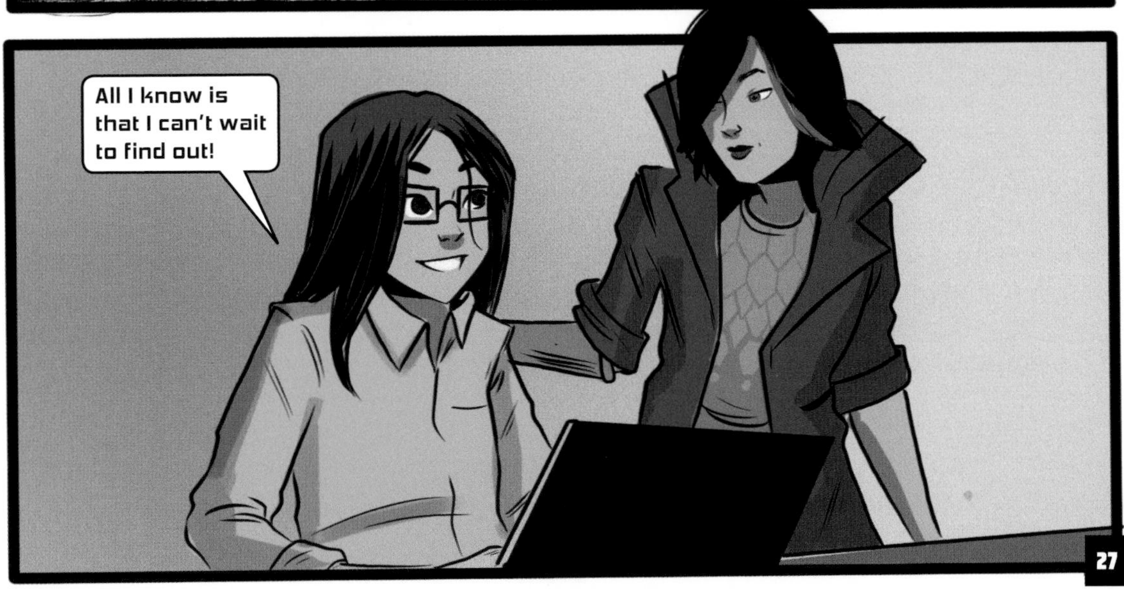
All I know is that I can't wait to find out!

MEDICAL ADVANCES

- Polio was once a common childhood illness. Lasting effects of the disease included loss of reflexes and muscle weakness. The first vaccine for polio was used in 1955. By 2000 the world saw a 99% reduction in polio cases.

- The first human organ transplant was done in 1954 with a kidney. Today doctors can transplant hearts, kidneys, livers, lungs, corneas, skin, valves, and more. Doctors in the future may be able to transplant a human head onto a different body.

- Obesity has become a big problem in developed nations. There has been a lot of medical research done to try to solve this problem. Some scientists are studying how genes affect weight. One day they may be able to use gene therapy to cure obesity.

- Doctors and researchers are also using gene therapy to treat cancers. By analyzing the genome of cancer cells, doctors can tell which cancer treatments will have a better chance of success.

- Sharing medical records between doctors and facilities has always been a challenge. Social media has provided inspiration to solve this problem. In the future, medical records may exist in web-based "clouds" that are accessible to medical professionals everywhere.

- 3-D printing of organs is an area that many doctors and scientists are interested in. However, another possibility is 3-D printed medications. This development would change the way medical drugs are sold. Patients may be able to print their own medications.

Many patients have a hard time remembering to take their medications. Companies have started selling pill bottles that glow when it is time to take a dose. In the future this information may be sent to your doctor so that he or she will know when patients are taking their medication.

The possibilities in medical robots are nearly endless. In the future robots may deliver supplies. They could serve as remote communications devices to connect patients and doctors. They could also serve vital roles in monitoring and enhancing physical therapy.

LUNA LI

Futurists are scientists who systematically study and explore possibilities about the future of human society and life on Earth. Luna proved herself to be brilliant in this field at a young age. She excelled in STEM subjects and earned her PhD in Alternative Futures from the University of Hawaii at Manoa. Luna invented a gadget she calls the Future Scenario Generator (FSG) that she wears on her wrist. Luna inputs current and predicted data into the FSG. It then crunches the numbers and creates a portal to a holographic reality that humans can enter and interact with.

antibiotics (an-tee-by-AH-tiks)—drugs that kill bacteria

bacteria (bak-TEER-ee-uh)—one-celled, tiny living things; some are helpful and some cause disease

clone (KLOHN)—organism with the exact same genes as the organism that produced it

cochlear implant (KOH-klee-ur IM-plant)—a small electronic device that is surgically put into a person's head; cochlear implants allow sounds to get to the brain

diagnosis (dy-ig-NOH-suhs)—a doctor's opinion about what caused a patient's problem

DNA (dee-en-AY)—material in cells that gives people their individual characteristics; stands for deoxyribonucleic acid

evolve (i-VAHLV)—when something develops over a long time with gradual changes

gene (JEEN)—unit of a cell that determines the characteristics an offspring inherits from its parents

genome (JEE-nome)—full set of genes in an organism

smallpox (SMAWL-poks)—a disease that spreads easily from person to person, causing chills, fever, and pimples that scar

vaccine (vak-SEEN)—a medicine that prevents a disease

virus (VYE-russ)—a germ that infects living things and causes diseases

Hartman, Eve. *The Scientists Behind Medical Advances.* Sci-hi Scientists. Chicago: Raintree, 2011.

Jackson, Tom. *Medicine and Health.* Redding, Conn.: Brown Bear Books, 2012.

Murphy, Jim. *Breakthrough!: How Three People Saved "Blue Babies" and Changed Medicine Forever.* Boston: Clarion Books, Houghton Mifflin Harcourt, 2015.

Schutten, Jan Paul. *Hello From 2030: the Science of the Future and You.* New York: Aladdin; Hillsboro, Oregon: Beyond Words, 2014.

INTERNET SITES

FactHound offers a safe, fun way to find Internet sites related to this book. All sites on FactHound have been researched by our staff.

Here's all you do:

Visit *www.facthound.com*

Type in this code: 9781491482643

Check out projects, games and lots more at
www.capstonekids.com

Super-cool stuff!